CW00495252

Soul Shock:
A Divine Love Story

By Jordan Green

ISBN: 9798761579934

www.youtube.com/jordangreenyt

Preface

Let me paint the picture for you: I'm sitting on top of a hill overlooking the best view that money can't buy. The Sun shares its warmth with me as I indulge in a peaceful meditation. This is precisely what I was told to do by my higher self, or my divine guides, or God- let's not get caught up in semantics. I fully embrace the chaos of my consciousness until I finally find stillness. In this transient tranquility, I present a simple question to the same higher power which has led me to this moment of inner harmony: "What is the next phase of my healing journey?" Almost instantaneously, I am given rather vague instructions: "Tell your story." Despite the lack of specificity, I intuitively know what this message means. And by the end of this book, so will you.

For some reason or another, you've been guided to read this book in much the same way that I've been guided to write this book. Throughout these pages, I aspire to build a bridge between my experiences and yours- a bridge constructed of compassion and understanding. Perhaps you are currently going through or have already gone through certain experiences that align with mine. Or perhaps you will in the future, and this book will serve as preparation for those experiences. In any event, I encourage you to absorb the book at a pace that's comfortable for you- particularly if you aren't accustomed to deciphering poetry. This may present itself as an *intensely* emotional read, as many emotions were expressed in the creative process.

This book is largely inspired by some of my favorite music projects (which I will list down below), so the book does not follow the chapter-by-chapter structure present in most traditional works of literature. Rather, the book is structured much like a concept album with its free-flowing nature and thematic uniformity. With that being said, you might find that listening to music helps enhance your reading experience. Here are some of the albums that I listened to (often obsessively) to put myself in the emotional space necessary to do my story justice:

1. *Freudian* - Daniel Caesar
2. *Blonde* - Frank Ocean
3. *When It's All Said and Done... Take Time* - Giveon
4. *IGOR* - Tyler, the Creator

These are only personal suggestions; feel free to listen to anything that makes you *feel* something. Or don't listen to anything at all. This book is meant to be a uniquely intimate experience for each reader. It's a source of healing for anybody willing to embrace their emotions, so try to find a safe space where you can experience your feelings thoroughly. The vast majority of this book was written in my car in various parking lots on the wrong side of midnight; that's my safe space. Find yours (if you haven't already), and let's embark on this tumultuous journey together.

Introduction

I was 19 years old when we met, and so was she. Up to that point, I had never had a girlfriend, I had never had sex (much less kissed a girl), and I had never fallen in love. Truth be told, I didn't even know what falling in love really meant. Growing up, I had opportunities to pursue romantic relationships with a few different girls, but I rejected every single one of them. For a while, I didn't know why I declined these invitations to intimacy. Seeing everyone else find love at such young ages made me feel extremely insecure about myself, and yet I still avoided relationships (and women) like the plague. And to make matters worse, I would always give the same excuse: "I'm not ready for a relationship."

At the time, I thought that I was just saying that to spare my admirers' feelings, but looking back on it there was a high degree of validity to that sentiment. Perhaps I subconsciously knew that I lacked the emotional maturity to handle the stresses that relationships bring, and I hid behind my inner truth without even realizing it. That's what my logical mind tells me in order to rationalize my actions, but in my heart I know that's just part of a much larger, less logical truth. Deep down, I always knew that there was someone out there waiting for me, and I didn't want to waste time entertaining girls who weren't her. Now I am acutely aware that this could be perceived as a limiting belief, but this clairvoyant hunch persisted throughout the entirety of my youth. Not only did I know that someone was waiting for me, but I knew that this special someone would be worth the wait.

With that being said, I can't remember any point in my childhood where I didn't have a crush on *someone*. Some years it would be a girl at my school; other years it would be a girl on the internet. But there was always someone, and there was always a reason why. In the same way that one girl's smile would leave me hypnotized, another girl's eyes would leave me mesmerized. As I grew older, I learned that personality is just as, if not *more* important than looks, so I began to take girls' inner traits into account as well. While one girl would captivate me with her kindness, another would solicit me with her sense of humor. But as I explained earlier, I never fully pursued any of these women because I knew that there was a girl out there that possessed the full package. I would occasionally have dreams about this girl, but I never knew exactly what she looked like. She adopted different physical forms from dream to dream, but there was one thing that remained constant throughout every dream: the way she made me feel. This mystery girl made me feel a feeling that I had never felt before. This sensation was beyond that of conventional childhood romance; it was a true understanding and acceptance of everything that I am- including all of my core wounds and hidden traumas. It was a feeling so intense that I don't ever recall exchanging any words with this mystery girl because words weren't necessary. The connection adequately spoke for itself. In retrospect, this feeling was the standard by which I assessed any potential partners, and if I'm being honest it still is. Unfortunately, I never really found someone who could make me feel the way that the girl in my dreams made me feel. That is, until I turned 19.

As I mentioned earlier, I had absolutely no dating experience at 19 years of age. I was insecure about my lack of experience, but my low self-esteem discouraged me from entering the dating world. And the longer I went without dating, the less experience I had relative to everyone else my age- which, in turn, made my self-esteem even worse. At a certain point, I identified the cycle that I was in, and I decided to end it once and for all. Because I wasn't in college (I dropped out right after I turned 19) and I didn't enjoy traditional social settings such as parties and clubs, my options for meeting women were very limited. Eventually, I resorted to dating apps (particularly Tinder), and thus began my journey into the wicked world of romance.

Initially, I had little to no success in the dating world. My lack of experience showed, as I never knew when or how to make a move. As pitiful as it sounds, holding hands with a girl was a *huge* accomplishment for me at the time. I didn't know the dynamics of casual relationships (which are exceedingly common on dating apps), and I didn't understand the various stages of dating- especially the infamous "talking stage." After two *miserable* attempts at dating, I quickly found myself back at square one: lonely, insecure, and desperately craving affection from a woman. After my second time being rejected and/or ghosted, I decided to take a little break from dating in order to focus on my career. By this point I had already started my YouTube channel ("Jordan Green"), and I had *extremely* large aspirations for it. But despite my dedication to my desires, I saw very little progress and my future seemed bleak. After a few months, I decided to distract myself from my own misery by getting back on Tinder. It's genuinely astonishing how *one* decision can completely alter the trajectory of your life. Had I not gotten back on Tinder when I did, you would not be reading this book right now. Nevertheless, I got back on Tinder and a few days later I matched with the girl who would ultimately become the inspiration behind this book. From that day forward, my life would never be the same again.

In my then 19 years of life, I had never hit it off with someone as well and as quickly as I did with her. It didn't take long for me to realize that she was different from any other girl that I had met up to that point. Initially, it was the quality of conversation that stuck out to me. While most girls would give me low-effort responses, she gave me elaborate answers while also showing just as much curiosity about me as I had about her. After about two days of texting her, I realized that we had quite a bit in common- so much so that I initially thought one of my friends was pranking me by pretending to be her. I was vegan, and she was vegetarian (or maybe pescatarian?). And not only that, but we had both made these dietary decisions within a few months of each other in the same calendar year (2017). We both had rather infuriating skin conditions. We both had to attend regular chiropractic sessions for one reason or another. We had a similar taste in music- with both of us liking Daniel Caesar in particular. But perhaps the most distinct of these commonalities was that we both saw angel numbers (specifically 111 and 1111). She was- up to that point- the *only* other person I had ever met that saw these numbers as frequently as I did. We even sent each other screenshots every time we saw one of those numbers, and it wasn't uncommon for us to exchange five to ten of those screenshots (each) in a single day.

As the days went on, we began texting more and more. Soon after we started talking, I went to Los Angeles for four days to film a few YouTube videos. But in spite of my commitment to my craft, I took *every* available chance that I had to talk to this girl. And the more we talked, the harder I fell for her. I told myself (and my friends) that I would remain level-headed and not catch feelings for her too quickly, but I never even stood a chance.

By the time I got back home to Dallas, we were texting every single day; we even held multiple conversations at a time across different apps. Soon after I got home, I decided to ask her out on a date, and she delightfully accepted my offer. While we were discussing our date via text, I mustered up the courage to call her so that we could break the ice in advance. I also wanted to confirm that she was actually a real person, and as fate would have it, she was. I called her a little after 10:00 PM, and we stayed on the phone until around 4:00 PM the following day. I had known this girl for all of one week, and our first phone call lasted *18 hours*.

A great way to examine the integrity of your connection with someone is to observe your perception of time when you're with them. I can tell you with wholehearted honesty that this 18 hour phone call felt like ten minutes to me. During that call, we somehow found enough time to iron out the details for what would be our first date, and so would be the beginning of my new life.

The day of our first date came, and I was *extremely* nervous. I made sure that I was well-groomed and well-dressed, and I picked her up from her house at around 6:30 that evening. I still remember the moment that I saw her in person for the first time. She walked out the front door, and everything seemed like it was going in slow motion. She gracefully trotted down the stoop, and she did a little jump off of the last step. Forgive me for my lack of an explanation why, but *that* was the moment that I truly fell in love with her. Although the Sun had long ago set, I could see her smiling face in the dim lighting of my car. My first observation upon seeing her in person was that she was even better-looking in real life than she was in her pictures. We gave each other a typical nervous first date hug, and then I gave her the flower bouquet that I had bought her- my signature move at the time. We went out to dinner at a nearby vegan restaurant (which is now permanently closed), and then we went and saw the movie "Bad Boys for Life." This presented me with the opportunity to hold her in my arms for the first time, and from that point on any semblance of doubt disappeared from my mind: she was the one. I knew it, and I felt it. I had caught feelings in the past, but this was different. This was almost too good to be true, but I knew it was real. And if my gut didn't confirm it, then seeing 1111 halfway through the movie certainly did (we both found this to be quite amusing).

After the movie, I drove her back to her place. The drive typically takes around ten minutes, but I made sure to drive extra slow so as to savor every single moment spent with her. I didn't want the date to end, and evidently she didn't either. I pulled up in front of her house at around 11:00 PM, and she didn't get out of the car until 2:00 AM. We sat in front of her house for three hours listening to the music playlist that she made for us (she had made a playlist full of our favorite songs prior to our date) and simply enjoying each others' company. We even found time to have a few thumb wars. No, this is not a sexual metaphor; we *literally* wrestled thumbs. And if my memory serves me well, I won every single match- though I'm sure she would dispute this claim.

Just like with our first phone call, those three hours flew by in minutes. This undeniably confirmed the magnitude of our connection, and it was the first time that I experienced a feeling like that which I felt in my dreams. And that's when it hit me: this girl wasn't just any ordinary girl: she was essentially every girl that I had ever liked put into one person. One could theorize that I subconsciously kept track of all of my favorite traits from every crush I ever had, and they all culminated in me finding this one girl who possessed *all* of said traits. Or one could argue that it was *her* I was looking for all along (hence, the dreams), and I was subconsciously looking for her in every other girl, but to no avail. Either way I knew that she was the one that I had so patiently waited for, and any resistance rooted in fear of being hurt again was promptly evicted from my mind that night.

After our date ended, we continued talking in the same way that we had before. We were as inseparable (via text and FaceTime) as our schedules would permit. We even made plans to see each other on Valentine's Day the following week. Everything was going absolutely wonderful- until it wasn't. One day, seemingly overnight, she became *extremely* distant. I texted her, but she didn't respond for hours. It got to the point where I was genuinely concerned for her safety, and I began to panic. I didn't want to seem needy or possessive, so I didn't express my concern to her. But it ate me alive all day. After about seven hours of silence, I saw that she was typing on Snapchat (a messaging app). I was equal parts relieved and anxious. I was relieved because I knew that she was okay, but I was anxious because I knew that her message would likely be related to us- and not in a good way. She sent her message, and I waited a couple of minutes to open it. In part because I didn't want to come across as desperate, but also because I was scared of what the message might say. I finally built up the courage to open it, and my heart and stomach dropped in unison. Her message read, "Sorry, I didn't mean to ghost you. Can I talk to you about something?" Although I was inexperienced, I did have experience with that heart-shattering question. In fact, *both* of the previous girls that I had "talked to" asked me the same exact question right before they ended things with me. Because of this, I had a general sense of what she was about to say, but that didn't lessen the impact of her next message by any means. I don't have the message committed to memory (thankfully), but the essence of it was her explaining how she wasn't ready for a relationship and that she would like to just be friends. I'm going to momentarily put my pride to the side and be honest with you: I broke down. I went for a late-night drive to gather my thoughts, but instead I was overwhelmed with emotion. The girl that I had been waiting for for the better part of *19 years* was suddenly out of my life. Or was she?

In that same message, she said that we could continue to hang out with each other, but we would have to do so as friends. I begrudgingly agreed, as I knew that I couldn't stand to lose this connection that I had so patiently waited for. A few days later, we went out as "friends" on Valentine's Day. To this day, I can confidently say that this was the best mistake I ever made. We met up at a local sushi restaurant, and I was pleasantly surprised to see that nothing had really changed. I thought that things would become awkward between us- especially given that it was the most romantic day of the year- but the energy was excellent. In fact, the energy was a little *too* excellent given the fact that we were "just friends."

We intended to just go out for lunch, as she had other plans later that evening. But after lunch, we ended up going to a nearby Target grocery store (at her request) so that she could show me all of the vegan snacks that they had. After that, we sat in my car, ate the snacks, and listened to music until it was time for her to go. I drove her back to her car which was still parked outside of the restaurant, but she didn't get out. By this point, I knew her well enough to know that she had no intentions of getting out of my car anytime soon, so I pulled into a parking space next to her car. While we were sitting in the parking lot, we held a deep discussion about mental health and how it affected us both. It was mostly a one-sided conversation, as I opened up to her about how miserable and depressed I was- particularly regarding my dissatisfaction with my YouTube content and the adverse effects that it had on my self-perception. For some reason, I got the sense that her ears were a safe space for my inner turmoil. And based on what she had previously told me, the feeling was mutual. This conversation only made our connection even more intimate, as she took the time to give me genuine, heartfelt advice on how I could overcome my depression in a natural manner. Perhaps the most impactful tip that she gave me was to open up to my YouTube supporters about my depression. Since then, I've used her advice to generate great success on YouTube, and for that I'm eternally grateful.

While we were talking, she pulled out her phone to send someone a message. Given the fact that she was already 30 minutes late for whatever she had planned that night, I concluded that she was cancelling her plans to spend the rest of Valentine's Day with me. Although I felt this to be a tad inappropriate given our status as friends, I decided to go with the flow. I was enjoying her company far too much to ask any questions, and the feeling was clearly mutual. After talking for a while, we decided to go to a nearby bookstore (also at her request) for reasons that have since eluded my memory. Nonetheless, we went to the bookstore and came out empty handed two hours later. We spent *maybe* 20 minutes of that time actively searching for books, while the rest of the time was dedicated to reading a "Would You Rather" book while laughing hysterically (much to the annoyance of everyone else nearby). In fact, the only reason why we left the bookstore at all was because they were closing for the night. We got in my car, and I drove her back to her car yet again. By this point, it was around 10:00 PM, so I was expecting her to go home (we had been out for around seven hours by this point), but she didn't even unbuckle her seatbelt. I parked in the spot adjacent to her car, and we sat there until 1:00 AM watching videos and listening to music- quite the day for a couple of "friends" who had only met a few weeks prior.

Initially, I figured that our friendly Valentine's Day date was somewhat of a fluke. That is, until we went on our third date. This time, we went to yet another vegan restaurant, then we went to Daiso (a Japanese dollar store), and then we went to an ethnic grocery store. While we were at Daiso, I noticed that she kept getting needlessly close to me. If I showed her something, for example, she would lean in excessively close as if to say, "hold me and don't ever let me go." Then while we were at the grocery store, she mentioned that it had been exactly one month since we had matched on Tinder. I found this to be a rather unusual thing to point out to a "friend" (especially given the context of the situation), but I simply brushed it off. We got our groceries (mostly consisting of different flavors of mochi), and we drove to a nearby parking lot. While we were sitting in the parking lot, I received a very clear and defined message from the same divine power that instructed me to write this book. This message presented itself as an unrelenting gut feeling that me and her were meant to be together, and I have *supreme* faith in the accuracy of my intuition. In retrospect, my intuition was indeed correct. However, it was (justifiably) misinterpreted by my rational mind. At the time, I thought my intuition was telling me that we were meant to be in physical union *forever*. In reality, it was only telling me that we were meant to be in physical union *during that season of our lives*. Unfortunately, this was a realization that I would later reach through the agonizing experience of separation, but I'll elaborate on that in the poetry portion of the book.

Although things appeared to be going great on the surface, I was still miserable deep down. Not only did I despise my position in life, but I despised the fact that the one person who I wanted to be with was keeping me an arm's length away from her heart. This created a great deal of anxiety within me, as her words didn't line up with her actions. On one hand, she *explicitly* stated that we could only be friends. But on the other hand, her actions indicated that she wanted us to be together just as badly as I did. In hindsight, I hypothesize that she subconsciously acted in ways that reflected her interest in me- even though she didn't intend to. In other words, she was probably largely unaware of her actions, but I sure as hell wasn't. I knew that our little arrangement was quickly approaching its expiration date, but I didn't yet love myself enough to let go of her- nor did I have the courage to make a move on her.

Nevertheless, this expiration date would come shortly after our fourth date. This wasn't because of anything that happened while we were hanging out (not to my knowledge, anyways). Our little meeting went quite well actually. She introduced me to an affluent part of the area that I still frequent with high levels of enthusiasm. While there, we sat in a Tesla (our collective dream car) for roughly an hour, we went out to eat, we grabbed some snacks from Target, then we had yet *another* jam session in the car. And to top it all off, I filmed a good portion of the date. I know it sounds like a peculiar thing to do, but she is actually the one who requested it. Prior to meeting, she told me that she wanted to create a little video montage- presumably to post on social media. With me being an up-and-coming YouTuber at the time, I jumped at the opportunity to give my camera some run. But I also had more personal intentions in mind. I wanted to record a few of our interactions so that I could analyze them to see if I was delusional about her liking me. And upon further analysis, I realized that I was not delusional in the slightest. After realizing that she did indeed like me, I decided to start making romantic advances towards her. This ultimately proved to be the turning point in our "friendship," as she slowly but surely began to distance herself as a result. As a knee-jerk response, I decided to push even harder- until I pushed a little *too* hard.

Once I recognized that she wasn't reciprocating my energy in the way that I had expected her to, I decided to send her a poem to express my regret over trying to pressure her into a relationship. Hours later, she responded by reiterating that we could only ever be friends, and that she had tried to be as clear as possible about that. Upon reading her message, I instantly knew that I had made a catastrophic mistake- one that I likely wouldn't be able to recover from. Although she didn't directly say it, I knew that I wouldn't be seeing much (if any) of her moving forward. This aforementioned poem- titled "I'm Sorry"- is the 11th poem featured in this book.

Since that dreadful day, we've had no physical contact whatsoever. We've had a few text exchanges throughout that time period, though none of them even remotely resemble a true conversation. For many months, my petitions to her decision to end our "friendship" were met with frigid silence. But although we weren't in direct communication, we did keep tabs on each other via social media. This was obviously much easier for her to do, as I was more consistent than ever on YouTube. But because I kept tabs on her, I was able to pick up on *any and all* evidence that indicated that she was keeping tabs on me (some of which I intend on taking to the grave with me). These signs ranged from subliminal social media posts, to her viewing my Instagram stories, to her applauding my spiritual growth during a brief text exchange (despite the fact that we hadn't communicated in months), to her adding mournful music to *our* playlist soon after this aforementioned exchange, to her outright telling me that she had watched one of my videos which included footage from that fourth date (the video has since been deleted out of respect for her). Some of these signs I found through intention, others I found through coincidence.

Nonetheless, I got the sense that she was having much more trouble letting go than she initially let on, and this only prolonged my own healing process. Every time I felt like I was ready to move on, I would see something that would set me back months at a time. In retrospect, I have no one to blame but myself for extending my healing journey, as I chose to keep tabs on her under my own free will. Nevertheless, I intentionally avoided going to her city (and all of its delicious vegan restaurants) for months on end so that I could avoid an inevitably painful chance encounter.

During this extended period of no contact, I began to have *extremely* vivid dreams about the two of us. The details and the overall context would vary from dream to dream, but the dreams would always end the same way: with her leaving me. This was an extremely difficult time for me, as I essentially relived the soul shock of losing her over and over again for months. I also began to see a multitude of different angel numbers every single day. These experiences inspired me to conduct my own research on the topic of *twin flames*.

To be as concise as possible, twin flames are said to be one soul split in half and placed into two separate bodies: the divine masculine and the divine feminine. Twin flames are an inherently controversial topic, and rightfully so. From the outside looking in, it appears to be an ideology rooted in the lack of reciprocity. From a mental and emotional standpoint, buying into this belief is one of the worst things you can do as it enables insecure attachment styles and limiting belief systems. Unfortunately, the belief was already there before I even knew what it was. It was conceived the moment I had my first dream about that mystery girl. The further I went down the rabbithole of the twin flame ideology, the more it resonated with me at an intuitive level. And as I explained earlier, I have unwavering faith in the accuracy of my intuition.

As I researched more about the concept of twin flames, I realized that the parallels between my findings and my fractured connection with this girl were astounding. Every time I tried to find a logical loophole to dispel the similarities, I would find a new perspective that transcended rationality. This was simultaneously terrifying and liberating. It was terrifying because I realized that my gut feeling wasn't lying and that this girl was placed in my life for a divine reason, but it was liberating because I no longer felt the need to find a logical explanation for why things transpired the way that they did. All of the answers lay right there in front of me, but it was entirely on *me* to figure out what to do with that information. Ironically, she was actually the one who introduced me to the concept of twin flames. I don't remember the exact context, but I do remember her telling me something about twin flames and the divine feminine during one of our overnight phone calls. However, this had little to no influence on my decision to research the twin flame ideology. This was just one of many synchronicities that I experienced throughout our time together, and these synchronicities still find their way into my life after all this time (particularly angel numbers). I like to think of them as little reminders to stay present and to remember the ultimate goal in all of this: unconditional self-love.

For those unfamiliar with the concept of twin flames, there are said to be multiple "stages" along the twin flame journey. Perhaps the most recognizable (and painful) of these stages is the "runner and chaser" stage. I could further expound upon this stage, but I believe the name adequately speaks for itself. In our case, I was largely the chaser, and she was largely the runner. But in retrospect, I've realized that we were *both* runners. In the same way that she ran from our seemingly divine connection, I ran from a deeper relationship with *myself*. Having her in my life gave me a sense of wholeness for the first time, and I grew extremely attached to said feeling. My mistake was in believing that she was the only potential source of wholeness in my life. What time has taught me is that this is a feeling that I can and should give to myself. I had to learn how to fill my own cup and transcend my inferiority complex. To this day I am still working on developing a stronger relationship with myself, but writing this book is certainly helping to accelerate that process. And I hope that my vulnerability can do the same for you. I hope that my story resonates with you such that you feel understood on your path to spiritual and emotional freedom.

Whether you believe in twin flames or not, heartbreak can be *extremely* isolating, and no one should have to endure such suffering in solitude. Through my writing, I hope to serve as a beacon of light for anyone trapped within the darkness of their own minds. If you are currently dealing with heartbreak and the ensuing soul shock, I am here to tell you that it does get better. *Time heals all wounds, but only via the power of true unconditional love for oneself.* There will be times when you think you've healed, but you later find that you were only caught in the eye of the storm. This is when patience comes into play. Don't cast judgement upon yourself for feeling the way that you feel- regardless of how much time has passed. Have faith in yourself, and have faith in the divine (whatever you believe that to be). As time goes on, the storm will weaken, and the Sun will shine its familiar rays directly into your soul.

This is *not* a manual on how to rekindle a romantic relationship with someone who is no longer in your life; this is a manual on how to rekindle your relationship with *yourself*. As I take you throughout my healing journey, give yourself a chance to reflect on each individual line, as it might help you identify inner emotional blockages that are holding you back from a deeper relationship with yourself. There will be ups and downs and twists and turns along your path, and it is only through self-love that you will ultimately make it to your destination. This is the most prominent lesson that she taught me- through both conversation and circumstance- and I am now passing this lesson on to you in the form of poetry and journal excerpts. But before you immerse yourself in this emotional experience, I want to share one piece of advice for anyone on their twin flame journey. This message was delivered to me directly from the divine, and I hope that it has such a profound impact on you as it did on me.

When you feel a deep yearning for your "twin flame," don't ignore it. Don't reject it. Don't fight it. Accept it for what it truly is. Your ego operates from a place of fear and lack, as its reference point lies outside of itself. When you feel that void within, your ego automatically looks outside of itself to fill it. This is the basis of the "runner and chaser" stage of the twin flame journey. The chaser believes that he or she must bring the runner "home" such that they complete each other and live in eternal bliss and harmony. However, this is a low-vibrational headspace to occupy, as it implies that you are your ego and not your soul. This is the very essence of the lack mindset, and this is also why you feel that yearning. That relentless desire is not telling you to bring your twin flame home to you. Rather, it is telling you to come home to yourself by embracing your true nature: infinite abundance and unconditional love. Your connection to your twin flame is divine in its own right, but it will never be stronger than your connection with yourself. Until you realize this, your twin flame will continue to run from you in the same way that you run from yourself. After all, they are your divine reflection. So the next time you feel that sense of yearning, don't run from it. Use it to guide yourself toward the relationship that you've always wanted: a relationship with yourself.

Love Is a Choice

Love is a choice
It is the internal voice
That reminds the soul
That it is complete and whole
Lost in your eyes
My love complete
Traverse the skies
Until we meet
On cloud nine
And stars align
The perfect constellation
Poetic proclamations
From the soul of my spirit
That voice; I can hear it

Constellations

Can't imagine my life
Without you
My future wife
No doubt that it's true
My ride or die
My shooting star
High in the sky
Yet never far
Illuminate my mind
With your heart
I never thought I'd find
A work of art
Like you
The FaceTime calls
The conversations
The withdrawls
And the constellations
In your eyes
Cosmic caterpillars
Give birth to butterflies
Souls metamorphosize
In the cocoon of
Our connection
As our love lingers
In conception

Connection

Body, soul, and mind
Connection
In your eyes, I find
Direction
Twin flame, my divine
Reflection

Butterfly

I've never felt this way before
Your soul assures
The deepest part of my core
That everything will be alright
As long as you're here
In my arms
A delicate butterfly
I'll do you no harm
I know you've been mistreated
Your mind led astray
Your heart defeated
Your love thrown away
But everything will be alright
As long as you're here
In my arms
I bought you a necklace
With a butterfly charm
I'll give it to you
When we make it real
When our love is born
And our hearts have healed

Toxic Love

The deepest sense of
Love I've known
Many years spent
On my own
Waiting for someone
Like you
And now my dreams
Are coming true
This divine reflection
Distorts my self-perception
Who am I without you?
Embrace the taste
Of toxic love
My favorite thing about you

Thumb Wars

Put your hand in mine
Let's not waste this time
We have together
Even though our
Souls are tethered
We won't be here forever
We wrestle thumbs
But secretly, I treasure
Your touch
Perhaps my love
Is far too much
But hand in hand
My master plan
Is in motion
This moment foreshadows
My divine devotion
To you
I won't let you win
I'll knock on that door
Till' you let me back in
I know that you'll come back
Or maybe I'm lost in my
Own state of lack
You run, I chase
Your endurance is admirable
But the thought of losing you
Is simply unfathomable

Trauma Bonding

I see the good
But feel the bad
When I'm with you
I wish we had
More time to heal
Before we met
If this is real
Then we should let
It flow
But first we must
Let go

Lost

Lost without your touch
Lost without your gaze
Lost without your energy
Lost within the days
I've spent without you
I can't quite explain it
But there's something about you
That reminds me of me
Ethereal reflection
That transcends
Material connection
Attachment sets me free
Attraction beyond superficiality
My soul loses its sense of reality
My problems don't exist
When I'm with you
These moments filled with bliss
Could this be true?

What Are We?

When I look into your eyes
I see more than a friend
When I look into your heart
I see the start, not the end
Of what we've come to be
Or what we'll never see
Together
Express this pain through
Carefully chosen letters
That tell you how much
I wish you were mine
See, connections like this
They're hard to find
Or maybe it's all in my mind
My intuition gives vision
To the blind
Reality we've created
Where lovers can only be friends
And nothing more

Love Again

Every time I'm in your presence
My heart beats faster than ever
Of love, you are the essence
I know one day we'll be together
Two broken souls
Fractured at the seams
I share with you all of my goals
Fears, memories, and outlandish dreams
I try to play it cool
But you give me butterflies
I turn into a fool
When you look into my eyes
I've never felt this way about any girl
If love is a flame
You're the spark that ignites my world
I just wish you felt the same
Or maybe you do?
Because these days you've got me confused
Am I your lover or your friend?
I know your heart has been battered and bruised
But through me those days have come to an end
If space is what you need
I'll build a rocket to show you the stars
Once your heart ceases to bleed
I'll use my love to heal the scars
But perhaps that's not my place
After all, we're just friends
Yet you extend a lover's embrace
After saying you weren't ready to love again

I'm Sorry

I'm sorry
I'm sorry I told you I would give you the space
You needed to heal
Only to continue my tireless chase
I can't force you to feel
The way that I do
Because truth be told
I'm still crazy about you
And your heart of gold
And your Hollywood smile
I'd be lying if I told you
It didn't take me a while
To accept that which is true
We can only be friends
Because in my past those words
Were the beginning of the end
Experiences that left my vision blurred
See, this isn't the first time
It's actually the third
That a potential relationship of mine
Turned on a dime
And I know that it's absurd
For me to compare you to them
Now I see with crystal clarity
That we can still be friends
Because you're a rarity
Chemistry that goes beyond
The periodic table
We share such a great bond
That we don't need a label
So with that being said
Let's just go with the flow
Don't get in your own head
Just continue to grow

Happy Birthday (Interlude)

"About two months ago, I found the girl of my dreams. I mean she's the full package: nice, smart, can cook vegan food, good taste in music, drop dead gorgeous, but above all, she inspires me to do better- and believe me, that's rare these days. Unfortunately, things haven't really worked out between us. She hasn't answered any of my texts in about a week, and maybe I'm being a little dramatic, but it's tearing me apart. I don't know where I went wrong. We have so much fun every time we get together, but when we aren't together, she becomes distant. My friends told me that I should drop her, but they don't understand- they'll never understand. In all fairness to her and them, I do admit that I have a tendency to catch feelings prematurely (ie. on the first date), but she matched my energy- until she didn't. It was almost overnight. One day we were FaceTiming each other for sixteen straight hours, and the next day she was telling me that she just wanted to be friends. And this was all within a week of our first date- which went absolutely amazing. We saw each other three times since then, and every time we saw each other, things were the exact same as they were on our first date. We would be out for hours on end enjoying whatever we were doing, and more importantly, enjoying each other's presence. I don't want to let her go, because truth be told, if I let her go, that's it for me. I'll never find someone like her. It wouldn't be fair for me to compare every future woman I date to her, but I know that that's exactly what will happen. I want to call her so badly and work things out, but I know she won't answer. And so now, on my 20th birthday- a day that's meant to be filled with celebration- my day has instead been filled with pain and suffering."

Soul Shock

All I desired
Gone in an instant
A connection so real
That I can't help but miss it
But what is there to miss?
Those fleeting memories
Of seeing my wish
Come true
In the form of you?
Twins of a flame
This warmth runs through
My soul
Illuminating my shadows
And bringing out my old
Traumas
But now you've left me
Stranded in the darkness
Running from my love
Just as I do
A divine reflection
This soul connection
From out of the blue
Perhaps we will
Find love again
Or perhaps this is
The end
A truth hidden by
The illusion of time
Shock of the soul
And torment of the mind

Broken

You taught me how
To fix myself
And then
You broke me

Morning

The stillness of
The morning
A broken heart
In mourning
Learn to love
This feeling
All a part
Of healing

Pyramids

That vast and vacant void
That you once filled
Those pyramids of pain
You helped me build
To be quite frank
These towers of trauma
Continue to consume me
These oceans in my eyes
Expressions of the true me
Your pants stained your Nikes
Your past stained my heart
Those tender nights
I'm thinkin bout you
And why we're still apart
Those pastel skies
Of pink + white
Take away the pain
While pixelated memories
Are all that remain
Of our love

Viridescent

My mind in the future
My soul in the present
My heart still stuck
On that night at Viridescent
That void that you left
Those visions forgotten
The restaurant gone
The food going rotten
That inner void looks to
A future unpromised
Where we both have everything
That we've ever wanted
I wish you were here
Sitting next to me
So that I could give you
The rest of me
The person that broke you
Can't heal you
Yet with every moment
I feel you within
Like two broken hearts
Trapped under the skin
That celestial bond
Gone with the wind

Limbo

Waiting for love
That never arrives
We've met each other
In previous lives
And now we're stuck
In limbo
Wasting days
That we could be
You want to get away
From me
Is my love no good?
I know that we should
Be together
And so do you
And in due time
It'll prove to be true

Sweet Dreams

Infiltrate my mind
In my slumber
Invasive dreams
And angel numbers
There's more to this
Than meets the sight
Use the shadows
To find the light

To My First Love

I deleted those videos
From the last time I saw you
But I never got rid of
That necklace I bought you
That I never got the chance to give you
I'm trying to let go of what we had
But you won't leave my head
Late nights spent awake in my bed
Then I fall asleep
And you visit me in my dreams
So I can lose you again
I've lost you a thousand times
In a million different ways
But secretly, I love these dreams
Because in them, we're together
And if you've moved on
I hope it's for the better
I hope that you don't feel the pain that I feel
I hope that you're able to heal
From the trauma of your past
The drama of the heart
We were moving too fast
And the blame is on me
I tried to hold on
When you needed to be free
I couldn't be alone
When we first started talking
I was glued to my phone
It was all day, every day
Together when apart
The day that I lost you
I also lost my heart
...

Those broken pieces scattered in the wind
The only way for me to heal
Was to look within
And wake up to the fact
That you didn't abandon me
I abandoned myself
What we had was bad
For my mental health
I gave you all of what was left of me
And you nourished it
And then you left
And you took custody of the happiness
That we created together
I paid my child support with the tears
That I shed when my soul ached for you
Tears that washed away the ego's paradigm
And reminded me that
Everything happens for a reason
These phases of life, they change like the seasons
They leave like autumn leaves
To make room for the winter
In which we met each other
A winter in which we almost became lovers
But "Almost is Never Enough"
Remember when we sang that together?
Man, how times have changed
And a future without you sure looks strange
But I have to focus on me
I have to love myself
So that I can be free
I need to feel what I felt with you
When I'm all alone
So I deleted your number
Out of my phone
I'm ready to put this love to the test
So from the depths of my soul
I wish you the best

Hurt People Hurt People

She was my medicine
Healing all the pain
She was my sunshine
Crying in the rain
Lost in my desires
Took but never gave
That everlasting fire
Extinguished by the wave
Of my insecurities
Intentions plagued
By impurities
You reap the energy
That you sow
End the cycle
By letting go

Still in Love

It's been
So long
Since I found love
At last
Yet it feels
So wrong
To leave you in
The past
I miss all
The memories
We never got
To make
With pleasure
Comes pain
A beautiful
Mistake

Meant to Be

I can't shake the feeling
That we're meant to be
Through months of healing
From you and me
I've learned to trust
My inner guides
Through love and lust
That great divide

Do You Still Think of Me?

Do you still think of me?
'Cause I still think of you
With every day that passes
My message heals the masses
But they don't have a clue
This pain I'm going through
Runs remarkably deep
I wonder if you'll ever take
That leap of faith
And reach out to me
Like I reached out to you
Unbeknownst to both of us
Those feelings weren't through
They live within me
As I write this
And I don't know
If I can fight this
For much longer
Because I want you back
But I never had you
I only had lack
I fell in fear of losing you
And here I am still choosing you
But are you choosing me?
Because if not, I need to know
So I can let you be
And you can set me free
To change the world on my own
Shall time reveal this great unknown?

Memories

The memories we made
My future in your eyes
The passion in our hearts
The chaos in disguise
Not ready for each other
This world can be so cruel
The pain you left me with
Became my source of fuel
That wasn't your intention
That I surely know
We needed time apart
To heal before we grow
So why can't I let go?

∞ (To Infinity and Beyond)

That tattoo on your wrist
A metaphor for memories
We've missed in speculation
Lifetime after lifetime spent
In painful separation
Perhaps you've run away
In pursuit of preparation
For our purpose
We came here to mend
The broken bonds of men
That tattoo on your wrist
A start with no end
Perhaps we'll have another chance
To lose that love again
Like that dreadful day you told me
We could only be friends

The Last Cry

Tears that could
Wash away shorelines
Desperation
Between my breath
The pain of
Death of love
That divine connection
From above
That left as quickly
As it came
And things will never
Be the same
These tears fall
Like autumn leaves
Like how you left
My soul to grieve
All alone
Those late nights
On the phone
Are what I miss
The most
Or maybe how
I'd hold you close
When it was time to go
Perhaps I knew
That any night
Might be our last together
These memories
Define my past
I'll cherish them forever

The Heart Wants What it Wants (Interlude)

"It's like I go through the five stages of grief every single day. I suppose that I should be thankful that I typically end my day on the acceptance stage. I've made my peace with the way things ended, but I also can't shake the feeling of her. We only knew each other for one month, and I've only seen her in person four times, yet she still lives rent-free in my mind. It's been so long since I last saw her that I've evolved into a completely different person. And yet I still find myself trapped on the same emotional roller coaster that I was on when I first started this journal. I've never really liked roller coasters because I don't like the feeling of not being in control of my situation, and these days it feels like I'm not even in control of my own mind."

Surrender

Surrender is the key
To a future between
You and me
We came here to awaken
Through memories forsaken
I have to let you go
If I want true tranquility
I hope that you'll join me
In expressing our abilities
To heal the masses
Hazel eyes hidden
Behind barriers; those glasses
Can't hide your inner truth
Or perhaps we were just
Two star-crossed youths
Who simply weren't ready
A truth we'll determine
When our souls are steady

Reunion

The further we get
The closer we are
Reunion is here
Yet you are so far
Faith in connection
Just follow the heart
This love a reflection
A brand new start
Do you feel the love
That I send your way?
'Cause I feel your love
With every day
That passes by
Eternal passion
The soul never lies

Tired

I'm tired of
Being tired of
Thinking about you
Yet I feel this connection
Like you're my reflection
I know that it's true
I'm tired of
Being tired of
Waiting for you
To come back
A state of being which
Perpetuates lack
I have to let go
I'm tired of
Being tired of
Pretending that we're
Not meant to be
I wish I was free
From this intuitive feeling
That interrupts
All attempts at healing
I'm tired of
Being tired of
Not knowing
If you feel the same
I wish I could ask
But I put on a mask
To hide the shame
I'm tired of
Being tired of
Wondering what
We could've been
The answer to that
Can only be found
By looking within

Closure

Focus on yourself
For closure is found
Through forgiveness
I lent you my heart
Foreclosure with love
As my witness
Fill your own cup
Until it runneth over
These late night drives
To bring myself closure
Set the intention
To lose my composure
The only way out
Is through
But that involves
Thinking about you
And I'm not prepared
For that kind of pain
But if I prolong it
I might go insane
I have to let go
In order to grow
And forgive myself
When my faith runs low
If this is the end
Then I bid you adieu
'Til we meet again
When I'm ready for you

Stuck

Freedom begets fear
Stuck in my ways
Too tired to move forward
I watch as the days
Pass me by
Wondering if this
Is all a lie
Time spent worrying
Is the ultimate waste
And that's why I'm done
With this tireless chase
Follow your reflection
And you'll never catch it
Reverse your direction
And become a magnet
Trust in your faith
And embrace the confusion
Live in the present
And release the delusion

Mirror

Through deep
Introspection
My perception
Much clearer
You were never
My reflection
You were only
The mirror

Acceptance

Finally free from
Fractured memories
Of what we could've been
I took the love I had for you
And I placed it within
In love with the thought of you
The end before the start
The time has come to let you go
'Til love do us apart

Letting Go

I wanted what I couldn't give
And what we had
You couldn't handle
My twin flame
An eternal candle
Extinguished in favor
Of inner fire
Become my best self
Ascend to higher
States of being
I slowly find my worth
Fulfill my purpose
And change this Earth
For the better
I wish you the best
Always and forever

Free

If you love someone
You set them free
What then becomes
Is meant to be
Love is freedom
Not adoration
Slay your demons
Enjoy creation
Don't hold hostage
Those expectations
Clear the blockage
Of old relations
Start anew
Within yourself
Know what's true
And say farewell
Butterflies fly
With joy they play
Attachments die
And there they stay

Grateful

I'm forever grateful for
Those late nights
In the car
Now I write
From afar
Those eternal
FaceTime calls
This internal
Overhaul
Those numbers
That we see
Your comfort
Around me
Those laughs
That we shared
Our paths
Rather rare
The memories
We made
The remedies
At bay

How Are You?

How are you?
Words I wish that I could say
With each and every passing day
These memories
They lead the way
I wonder
How you feel
Did losing me
Help you heal?
Or was it all in vain?
Did the same waves of pain
That drowned me
Carry you to shore?
I hate that we
Don't talk anymore
'Cause if we did, I would ask
How are you?
I truly want to know
I want to see you happy, and
I want to watch you grow
But sometimes, the purest
Act of love
Is the act of letting go
A hard pill to swallow
And the road to acceptance
A hard path to follow
But step by step
I'll make my way
And if we meet again someday
I'll ask
How are you?

Printed in Great Britain
by Amazon

75358409R00032